C O F F E E   W I T H

Shakespeare

S T A N L E Y   W E L L S

F O R E W O R D   B Y   J O S E P H   F I E N N E S

DUNCAN BAIRD PUBLISHERS

LONDON

Coffee with Shakespeare
Stanley Wells

Co-written with Paul Edmondson

First published in the United Kingdom and Ireland in 2008 by
Duncan Baird Publishers Ltd
Sixth Floor, Castle House
75–76 Wells Street, London W1T 3QH

Conceived, created and designed by Duncan Baird Publishers

Managing Editors: Peggy Vance and Gill Paul
Co-ordinating Editor: James Hodgson
Editor: Susannah Marriott
Assistant Editor: Kirty Topiwala
Managing Designer: Clare Thorpe

British Library Cataloguing-in-Publication Data:
A CIP record for this book is available from the British Library
ISBN: 978-1-84483-576-8
10 9 8 7 6 5 4 3 2 1
Printed in China

Publisher's note:
The interviews in this book are purely fictional, while having a solid basis in
biographical fact. They take place between a fictionalized William Shakespeare
and an imaginary interviewer.

CONTENTS

Foreword by JOSEPH FIENNES

Who was William Shakespeare? There are as many theories as there are academics, as many factions as there are experts. When I was preparing to play him in the film *Shakespeare in Love*, my starting point was that he was an incredible observer of the people around him, soaking up their characteristics like blotting paper. The key is that Will Shakespeare was Everyman: politically his views ranged across the board; in religious matters he was non-committal; sexually he was able to inhabit all points of view. He could deal with everyone from street urchins to monarchs, and he had the same problems as his characters. Being aware of his own doubts and contradictions made him intensely human.

One of my favourite speeches is "The Seven Ages of Man" from *As You Like It*, in which he describes the parts we all play through our lives – from mewling infant through lover, soldier and wise man to second childhood. Shakespeare's canon seems to reflect the stages of his own life, from the brilliantly crisp verse of *Romeo and Juliet*, through the middle difficult period of *Measure for Measure* and the man suffering from depression in *Hamlet*, and then the ebullience and transcendence of *The Tempest*. His life is set out for us in his works, in the same way that a chronological exhibition of Rembrandt's portraits, with their shimmering beauty and extraordinary vision of human frailty, would chart the progress of that artist's life.

Despite the huge thrust of technological advance since the Elizabethan era, the human condition Shakespeare wrote about remains timeless. We still fall in love and get angry and avaricious; we are materialistic or fanatical or seek spirituality.

Here was a man who understood all the pain of being human, yet loved life and humour and fun. Put simply, he was one of the greatest-ever literary humanists.

INTRODUCTION

Over the past four centuries, Shakespeare's iconic
status as a poet and dramatist has come to represent
what it means to be a genius, and his words have
provided a language of self-expression for every
human emotion. Shakespeare is cited as an authority
in moral, political and cultural contexts that even
he could never have dreamed of. His very name can
stimulate approval, challenge, argument, lunacy,
brilliance and, occasionally, especially among
schoolchildren, boredom. Shakespeare's legacy
represents more than the story of a life and its age:
it has dominated artistic and cultural endeavour in
every generation that has followed him.

What would it be like to meet Shakespeare? What
kind of man was he? What would we most like to ask
him? How would he reply? These are some of the

questions that faced us in undertaking this project, and percolated through it as the coffee brewed.

First, what tone of voice would be appropriate for the world's greatest writer? Clearly he could not speak in blank verse, and we had no wish to invent a fustian pseudo-Shakespearian lingo full of arch archaisms. He should, we decided, speak in an informal, friendly, unobtrusively modern fashion, which might incorporate a few submerged allusions to his work. We wanted him to sound good-humoured and unpompous, and not to take himself too seriously, because this is how we imagine he really was. We wanted him to come across as a thorough-going professional, a good colleague, a poet with his feet on the ground, but also justly proud of his professional achievements. We envisaged a degree of nostalgia appropriate to a man at the end of his life, and this allowed us to colour his responses with a human but never sentimental perspective. We saw him as a man of fundamental humility. A working man, practical in his attitudes to life and devoted to his family.

By necessity, there is a considerable element of interpretation in this book. The recorded facts about Shakespeare's life are patchy, leaving much to be imagined. In the interview that follows the biographical overview here, we have tried be true to the known facts as much as possible, and to fill in the gaps with reasonable conjecture. We have tried also to humanize the record – to make Shakespeare sound like the deeply thoughtful, wise, non-judgmental, humorous, sweet-natured and immensely sympathetic person that we believe him to have been.

WILLIAM SHAKESPEARE (1564–1616)
His Life in Short

A hush has descended on the Globe Theatre. The
packed audience of three thousand – lords, ladies,
gentlemen, merchants, tradesmen, sailors, lawyers,
servants, apprentices, schoolboys, prostitutes,
brothel keepers and beggars, many of whom have
paid only one penny to stand as "groundlings" in
front of the stage – are watching a brand-new play
in broad spring daylight. Richard Burbage enters
as the old King Lear. In his arms is his daughter,
Cordelia, played by a boy actor. Burbage fills the rapt
silence with sounds of torment even more painful
than his cries of madness on the heath an hour or
so earlier. His beloved Cordelia is "dead as earth".
Nothing as unremittingly bleak has ever been seen
on the English stage. Departing radically from

previous tellings of the story, William Shakespeare, the play's 42-year-old author, has been brave enough to let Cordelia die. By so doing, he has raised stark questions about the nature of existence, questions raised afresh each time *King Lear* is performed. Arguably the greatest of Shakespeare's plays, *King Lear* is also one of humanity's finest artistic achievements.

But who was Shakespeare, and how did he acquire such a brave, radical and questioning outlook? Many misguided people devote their lives to arguing that the William Shakespeare of Stratford-upon-Avon did not write the works attributed to him. Bizarre quests to ascertain who wrote his plays started in the late 18th century, and it sometimes seems that any other candidate will do, provided that he or she is either an aristocrat or university-educated. It is too readily assumed that little is known about Shakespeare's life. Inevitably there are gaps, but there is also much documented information.

The salient biographical facts are as follows. William Shakespeare was christened on 26 April 1564 in Holy Trinity Church, Stratford-upon-Avon, a prosperous market town of about 1,800 inhabitants. William was the third child and eldest son of John Shakespeare (before 1530–1601) and Mary Arden (d. 1608), who married in 1557. William's two elder sisters, Joan (born 1558) and Margaret (1562–63), died in infancy. His brother Gilbert was born in 1566 (d. 1612), another Joan in 1569 (d. 1646), Anne in 1571 (d. 1579), Richard in 1574 (d. 1613) and Edmund, who became an actor, in 1580 (d. 1607).

John Shakespeare was a glover and a whittawer, a trader in white leather. He served on the town council, in 1561 and 1563 becoming a Chamberlain, who had charge of borough property and finances, and in 1568 rising to Bailiff, the chief official. During his year in office as Bailiff, two professional playing companies acted in Stratford for the first time: the Queen's Men and the Earl of Worcester's Men. John Shakespeare was prosecuted for illegal wool dealing and for charging too much interest on a loan, but in 1571 he was elected Chief Alderman and served as a justice of the peace and Deputy Bailiff. In 1596, he was granted a coat of arms, officially making him (and successive eldest male heirs) a gentleman. He took the family motto *Non sanz Droict* ("Not Without Right").

On 28 November 1582, John's son William married Anne Hathaway (?1555–1623) from the nearby village of Shottery – by special licence from the Bishop of Worcester, since she was already three months pregnant. Their daughter Susanna (1583–1649) was followed two years later by twins – a son, Hamnet (d. 1596), and a daughter, Judith (d. 1662).

There is virtually no documentary evidence relating to William Shakespeare from 1585–92, which has led to this period being known as the "lost years". He appears again in 1592, in a book ostensibly written on his deathbed by the popular writer Robert Greene (1558–92) (its authorship is disputed). It refers to "an upstart crow" who thought himself "the only Shake-scene in a country". Shakespeare's three plays based on the reign of Henry VI were proving immensely successful by this time, and the reference suggests professional jealousy. Shakespeare's name first appeared in print in the following year, 1593 (the year that saw the murder of fellow playwright Christopher Marlowe), on the title page of the erotic narrative poem *Venus and Adonis*. This was dedicated, like *The Rape of Lucrece* in 1594, to Henry Wriothesley, third Earl of Southampton (1573–1624). The two poems went through many editions before

1616 and were Shakespeare's most successful printed works in his own time.

Shakespeare's career as a playwright coincided with the rise of professional theatre. The first important building dedicated to the performance of plays, the Theatre, was established in Shoreditch, London, in 1576 by James Burbage (1531–97). His son Richard (c.1568–1619) became Shakespeare's leading actor and the first to play Richard III, Hamlet, Othello and Lear, among other roles. In 1595, Shakespeare was listed as a joint payee of the Lord Chamberlain's Men for performances at court, which suggests that he was a shareholder in the company. When not appearing before Queen Elizabeth I (1533–1603), the company performed mostly at the Theatre until its land lease expired in 1597. In the spring of that year, Shakespeare purchased the great house of New

Place in Stratford-upon-Avon. We do not know exactly how much he paid for it, but it was certainly not the often-cited £60 and could have been as much as £120 — at a time when the annual salary of a Stratford schoolmaster was some £20. The Lord Chamberlain's Men performed at the Curtain on the north side of London's River Thames until 1599, when the Globe Theatre was built by using the timbers of the Theatre transported to the south bank. When theatres were closed because of often devastating outbreaks of plague, the companies toured the provinces.

Shakespeare is listed among those who evaded tax payments in 1597, while he was living in the Bishopsgate area of London, and again in 1598. The only letter that survives either to or from Shakespeare also dates from that year. It was penned by Richard Quiney (before 1577–1602), a Stratford man, and requested a loan of £30, probably on behalf of the people of Stratford. We do not know whether Shakespeare lent him the money. That same year, a literary chronicler and clergyman Francis Meres (1565–1647) compared Shakespeare to Ovid (Shakespeare's favourite writer), listed twelve of his plays (including the still lost *Love's Labour's Won*) and praised "his sugared sonnets among his private friends". Around 1599, one William Scott produced a university dissertation entitled *A Model of Poesie* which includes the earliest known, albeit short, literary criticism of Shakespeare. Scott quotes from *The Rape of Lucrece* and *Richard II*, though without naming their author.

The year 1601 saw the ill-fated rebellion against the monarch by the Earl of Essex, whose supporters paid the Lord Chamberlain's Men to perform *Richard II* in order to galvanize public opinion on the eve of the attempted coup. The rebellion failed, and members of the company gave evidence at the subsequent hearings in the court known as Star Chamber, which dealt with sedition and public disorder. Essex was beheaded. The Earl of Southampton was imprisoned in the Tower of London (with his cat), but released soon after James I succeeded Elizabeth, in 1603.

In 1602, Shakespeare bought 107 acres of land in Old Stratford for £320. During that year, John Manningham (d. 1622), a law student, saw an early performance of *Twelfth Night, or What You Will* at Middle Temple Hall in London and recorded a humorous anecdote about Shakespeare and Burbage arranging a post-show assignation with the same woman (see page 72).

On the accession of James I in 1603, the Lord Chamberlain's Men became the King's Men, and

Shakespeare and some of his fellows were granted scarlet cloth to wear in the coronation procession of 1604. The playwright's greatest financial investment came the following year, when he paid £440 for a half share in the Stratford tithes, an annual tax payable to the church (from which he might expect to make about £60 a year).

The only grandchild Shakespeare knew – Elizabeth, daughter of Susanna and the physician John Hall – was born in 1608 (d. 1670), the year that Shakespeare's mother died. *Shakespeare's Sonnets*, a collection of poems written over many years, was published in 1609. In this year the King's Men acquired the Blackfriars Theatre (a former monastery), which seated about six hundred. Smaller than the Globe, this was an indoor venue, which meant that plays performed here could use lighting and special effects. In the final years of his career,

Shakespeare collaborated with John Fletcher (1579–1625) on *Cardenio* (lost), *All is True* (also known as *Henry VIII*) and *The Two Noble Kinsmen*.

Our only surviving record of words directly spoken by Shakespeare dates from a court case of 1612. An apprentice, Stephen Belott, took action against his father-in-law, Christopher Mountjoy, over failure to deliver his marriage settlement, promised in 1604. Shakespeare, as go-between, had helped to arrange the match. He declared in court that he had known the men "for the space of ten years or thereabouts", and that he regarded Belott as "a very good and industrious servant" to whom Mountjoy had shown "great good will and affection". The case was settled in Belott's favour.

A year later, Shakespeare bought a gatehouse near the Blackfriars Theatre for £140, and for the next two years was involved in controversies relating to land enclosure in Stratford. His daughter Judith married Thomas Quiney (?1589–1662/3) in February 1616, and soon afterwards Shakespeare, perhaps mistrusting his new son-in-law, altered his will (signed on 25 March) to protect Judith's interests. We do not know the cause of Shakespeare's death. The bulk of his estate went to Susanna. Anne Shakespeare was specifically bequeathed "the second-best bed". Judith received £100 as a marriage settlement, the interest on £150 as long as she was married, and a "broad silver-gilt bowl". His granddaughter inherited the rest of his plate. William Walker, his young godson, received twenty shillings in gold, while Thomas Coombe, a Stratford friend, was bequeathed Shakespeare's sword. His fellow actors Richard Burbage, John Heminges (1566–1630) and Henry Condell (1576–1627) were left money to buy mourning rings. Burbage died in 1619, but the other two worked hard to publish a collection of Shakespeare's plays (about half of them for the first time), which appeared in 1623. This is the greatest of Shakespeare's legacies.

William Shakespeare was buried on 25 April 1616 in Holy Trinity Church, Stratford-upon-Avon, where his grave can still be seen in the sanctuary. Nearby are the font in which he was probably baptized, and the weird and wonderful misericords (carved wooden choir stalls) which, together with stained-glass windows and wall paintings that no longer survive, would have informed his earliest imagination. His epitaph reads:

Good friend, for Jesus' sake forbear
To dig the dust enclosèd here.
Blessed be the man that spares these stones,
And cursed be he that moves my bones.

Above the grave is a bust by the Dutch craftsman Geerhart Janssen. An inscription in Latin compares Shakespeare to the giants of classical literature, echoed in English by the claim that he was a great writer. This bust, together with an engraving of Shakespeare by Martin Droeshout (another Dutchman) which appeared at the front of the First Folio, provide the best-surviving likenesses.

Shakespeare's direct family line died out in 1670 with his granddaughter Elizabeth. Descendants of Shakespeare's sister, Joan, lived in part of the house now known as Shakespeare's Birthplace until the early 19th century.

So much for the facts. The rest of Shakespeare's biography is based on reasonable surmise. The school records do not survive, but as a Bailiff's son William would have been able to attend the local grammar school free of charge. His work bristles with the effects of this kind of education. Latin and Greek literature, as well as rhetorical figures, were drilled into pupils; days were long and holidays few. Although Shakespeare did not go to university, he would have left school around the age of fifteen with as much knowledge as a Classics graduate leaving university today. He could understand Italian (the source for *Othello* was only available in Italian at the time) and he could write French (which he uses in *Henry V*). He would have had, by law, to attend the Protestant church every Sunday, though it is possible he had Roman Catholic sympathies.

As for what Shakespeare was doing between the years 1585 and 1592, there are numerous theories. At first, very likely, he was learning to make white leather and gloves in his birthplace and supporting his young family. We do not know how much time he spent travelling or in Stratford or London (the journey took two or three days each way). He did not own property in London until towards the end of his life, and it is likely that he returned to Stratford to write during Lent and at other times when the theatres closed: he is a complex, literary writer and would have needed his books close to hand as he composed

Commendatory verses in the First Folio include those by Shakespeare's old friend and rival Ben Jonson (1572–1637) saying that he was "not of an age, but for all time" and naming him the "sweet swan of Avon". Comparing him to classical writers, Jonson began to establish Shakespeare as England's pre-eminent national poet. In 1661, the vicar of Stratford-upon-Avon, the Rev. John Ward (1629–81), made a note that he must visit the then 76-year-old Judith Quiney and talk to her about her father. She died before Ward got around to it, a failure that surely constitutes one of the greatest of all literary-biographical misses.

———

Applause now encircles the Globe Theatre stage. *King Lear* has finished. New words never before heard in English have been spoken. The play, like all Shakespeare's output, has displayed elements of both comedy and tragedy. The audience exits, then as now, stunned, shocked, moved, satisfied and exhausted on a profound emotional and physical level. Shakespeare was probably there too. He knew that he was famous in his own lifetime. It took posterity – the successive reading, editing and performance of his works – to make him a legend.

NOW LET'S START TALKING ...

Over the following pages, William Shakespeare engages in an imaginary conversation covering fifteen themes, responding freely to searching questions.

The questions are in green italic type; Shakespeare's answers are in brown type.

(UN)WILLINGLY TO SCHOOL

In Shakespeare's time, Stratford-upon-Avon in Warwickshire had around 2,000 inhabitants, a substantial number when the population of London was no more than 200,000. Situated on the River Avon, this market town was governed by a body of councillors and aldermen, led by the Bailiff. They sat in the Guildhall, which was part of the same building as the grammar school and adjoined the Guild Chapel. These buildings still stand, as does the impressive Holy Trinity Church. The school had a generous endowment and employed a series of Oxford graduates as its teachers. Its records do not survive, but there is no reason to doubt that Shakespeare was a pupil. The interview takes place in a former inn next door to Shakespeare's birthplace.

Good morning, Master Shakespeare! I hope you are comfortable here on your home territory. No doubt you remember this room.

Well, yes, it certainly seems familiar, but I can't exactly place it.

In your day, it was the taproom of the inn known as The Maidenhead. And you were born in the upstairs room next door!

I see — it was a bit different in my time! Who lives in the place now?

It hasn't been lived in for well over 150 years. It was bought for the nation in 1847 and is kept up by the Shakespeare Birthplace Trust, along with several other houses around the town that belonged to members of your family. They attract many hundreds of thousands of visitors every year.

Good Lord! Why's that?

Surely you realize that you are one of the most famous writers ever to have lived? Your plays are performed all over the world in hundreds of languages – in heavily adapted versions as well as exactly as you wrote them. Biographies of you stream from the presses, your plays and your life story are endlessly studied, and people regard you as a great thinker as well as a great playwright.

Whatever are you talking about? How can I possibly be more famous than Ovid – or Plautus, whose play *The Menaechmi* I adapted as *The Comedy of Errors*? Not to mention the great Geoffrey Chaucer and my friend Ben Jonson, who thinks so highly of himself, and poor Christopher Marlowe, who came to such a dreadful end in Deptford?

It's true, I assure you, your reputation is unparalleled. That's why I've come to talk to you today.

That calls for a drink!

What will you have? How about a coffee?

A cup of sack would be very welcome.

I'll send across the road for something to quench your thirst ... Now, sir, I'd like to ask you quite a few questions. Let's start with your early life here in Stratford-upon-Avon. Was this a good place for a writer to be brought up?

It gave me an excellent start in life because I got
such a good education at the grammar school. It
was rigorous, and we worked most days of the year,
starting before dawn in the winter and not getting
back home till the early evening. But although I
may have crept unwillingly to school, I appreciate
what it did for me. Most of my teachers were Oxford
graduates, and I owe them a lot – mainly because
of the training they gave me in Latin literature and
speech-making. From the age of about eight we
had to speak nothing but Latin in the classroom.
We had to translate verse and prose both from and
into Latin, write Latin prose and verse, write letters,
debate among ourselves and make speeches in the
language. I learned how to use scores of figures of
speech with Greek names – stychomythia, epizeuxis,
antanaclasis, zeugma, isocolon. Later I scattered
my writing with them, especially when I was starting

out as a playwright. I came to feel that this sort of thing was over-formal, but it helped the actors to learn the lines. There's a little scene in one of my comedies – *The Merry Wives of Windsor* – in which I show myself being put through my paces by the Latin teacher.

Argument and debating were especially useful for a budding playwright – they taught me to see both sides of a question. And we read some superb literature. My favourite was Ovid, especially the *Metamorphoses*. Such wonderful stories! I used some of them in my plays. In one of my first, *Titus Andronicus* (Ben Jonson became very jealous of its success!), I actually make one of the characters bring the book on stage. Then there are the historians and playwrights. There was a lot of public interest in classical civilization then, as you can tell from the plays that people like John Lyly and Kit Marlowe and George Peele and Tom Kyd were writing, especially during my early years in the theatre — stuffed with Latin quotations and references to Roman and Greek myths and history. Reading and acting Plautus and Terence at school gave me useful lessons in putting comedies together, and although Seneca can be a bit heavy, he taught me a great deal about tragedy.

Did you read much away from school?

Yes. Although my mother couldn't write much, she was quite a keen reader, and some of the townspeople were generous in lending their books, so I got to know a lot of poetry, history and old tales. Mostly, though, they owned religious books, some in Latin and even Greek — I was never much good at Greek, Jonson would tease me mercilessly about that! And

I learned a lot at church. Having to go to services every Sunday and often on weekdays too, we came to know the Bible well. And some of the sermons were powerful, if a bit long for us youngsters.

PLAY THE MAN I AM

Much of what Shakespeare says in the following
exchange about his early interest in the theatre
and about his youth and courtship (including
the information about his marriage) is based
on documented fact or reasonable conjecture.
However, we have no certain knowledge of how
he began his career as either an actor or a writer.
At school he would have been required to write
both factually and imaginatively, in both English
and Latin. He may well also have acted – for
example, in comedies by the Roman dramatist
Plautus. It seems highly likely that Shakespeare
wrote both prose and verse for his own pleasure,
but except for the sonnet (Number 145)
mentioned in this dialogue, no early writings
are known to have survived.

There were no theatres when you were a boy, not even in
London. Were you able to see English plays all the same?

Most of the great lords kept companies of players,
and they would often tour around. I loved hearing the
drums and trumpets that meant the actors were in
town, with their wagons and horses. It was especially
exciting in the year my father was Bailiff, when I was
four. The players had to apply to him for permission
to perform in the Guildhall. And he took me to see
them. There we were in the front row, he wearing
his alderman's red robes, and I in my best clothes,
loving every minute of it! The plays themselves were
nothing special, and they were far shorter and had
fewer characters than when I started to write, but
some of the acting was really good, especially by the
comics. When I was older, I saw Richard Tarlton, the
Queen's favourite. I'd like to have written a part for

him, but he died in 1588, just before I started writing plays. He was only about 40, poor fellow. Some of our family's friends put on plays too, like Davy Jones – a nice man, married a relative of my wife's. Around the time I got married, he persuaded the town council to part with thirteen shillings and fourpence so that he could put on a play at Whitsuntide. I'd developed a taste for acting at school, so I helped him by taking one of the bigger parts and began to realize that this was the life for me.

You married around this time didn't you? That was rather early in life.

Yes, I was only 18 – most unusual! And Anne was 26. To be honest, she was already pregnant. We were lucky not to have to appear before the ecclesiastical court. That would really have upset my mother. And we had to get a special licence from the Bishop of Worcester.

Had you already started writing by then?

I was always scribbling away, poems mostly, but even then I had ideas for plays. I was a quiet, observant sort of lad, and I loved listening to people talk and watching how they behaved. There were interesting characters around the town – people like old Bill Greenway the carrier, who would go up and down to London with his horse and wagon, twice a week sometimes, carrying letters and bringing back supplies. But I tore up everything except one poem which got printed much later, in my volume of sonnets. Sentimental of me, but it's a love poem in which I pun on Anne's surname, Hathaway – "hate away". The last lines are:

"I hate" from "hate away" she threw,

And saved my life, saying "Not you".

Most ingenious! So what happened after you married?

It wasn't an easy time. We lived with my parents.
As you'll have seen, the house wasn't tiny, but with
three younger brothers – Richard, Gilbert, little
Edmund (he was always my favourite) – and my sister
Joan, there was no room to spare. And our Susanna
arrived within six months. Not much money, either
– my father's business as a glover wasn't doing
well, so although I should have liked to have gone to
university, I had to help him instead. Within a couple
of years we also had the twins, Hamnet and Judith.
Knowing I really wanted to act and to write, I became
frustrated and depressed. Then, by a stroke of luck,
when the Queen's Men came to Stratford in 1587

they were one man short. I had the nerve to offer to fill the vacancy, and in desperation they hurriedly recast the play to give me a tiny part. They liked what I did, and asked if I'd join them as a bit-player. I could see there was no future for me in Stratford, and so could Anne, so after (as you may imagine) much heart-searching, we agreed I should take the plunge. I hated leaving her and the children, but my imagination was bubbling over and the opportunity seemed too good to miss.

I made my living as an actor at first, moving from one company to another as the need arose. It was excellent experience, not only in acting but also in the business side of theatre – I found I had a talent for that – and it brought me in touch with people of all kinds, from beggars and servants to the aristocratic families whose houses we often acted in. And I started to write plays. My first was *The Two*

Gentlemen of Verona — do you know it? A modest effort, based on an Italian story, but one of the comic actors in the company had a sweet little dog — a border terrier called Crab — and I wrote scenes for them together, and audiences loved them both.

BY MY TROTH, WELCOME TO LONDON

The period between the birth of Shakespeare's
twins in 1585 and his emergence on the London
theatrical scene, evidenced by an allusion in
the pamphlet *Greene's Groatsworth of Wit* in
1592, is the most poorly documented part of
Shakespeare's life, often referred to as "the
lost years". It has been conjectured, variously,
that he worked in a lawyer's office, joined the
army (like Ben Jonson), served as a sailor, or
worked as a schoolmaster. These years saw a
rapid development in London's theatrical life.
We don't know how, when or where Shakespeare
began to act and write, but since Greene's
allusion suggests professional jealousy, it must
have been well before 1592.

Touring the provinces is all very well, but real theatres were already going up in London, weren't they? Surely that was where you most wanted to act?

That's right. There'd been a playhouse called the Red Lion in Stepney in 1567, just three years after I was born. But it only lasted a few months, and it wasn't till 1576 that James Burbage built the Theatre in Shoreditch. His son Dick became my closest professional friend. After that, theatre took off as a major industry. There were many obstacles, especially from the city fathers, a puritanical lot – which is why playhouses had to be built outside the official City boundaries. But the Queen and most of her courtiers loved plays, so to get round the bans we subscribed to the fiction that the performances we gave in public were only rehearsals for when we appeared at court – at places such as Whitehall Palace or Hampton

Court. The Queen never came to see us on our home ground, of course, though many of her courtiers did. We were well paid for court performances – and it was excellent publicity. They used to boast about it on the title pages of plays when they were printed. On *King Lear* it said, "As it was played before the King's Majesty at Whitehall upon St Stephen's Night in Christmas Holidays" – that's because court performances were usually given during the holiday periods. By then King James was on the throne.

You mentioned obstacles. What others were there besides the opposition of the city fathers?

The theatre was a heavily regulated business. All companies had to have the patronage of a member of the nobility or the royal family, otherwise the actors would have been classed as rogues and vagabonds

– hardly a fit term for such respectable people as my colleagues John Heminges and Henry Condell, who both became churchwardens. Then there was censorship. We had to submit all our plays to the Lord Chamberlain. He'd make sure that they didn't touch on anything that might be offensive to the government or the Church. Sometimes he was not as careful as he should have been. Ben Jonson got thrown into jail in 1597 because of a row over a play called *The Isle of Dogs* which he wrote with another friend of mine, Thomas Nashe – a wonderful writer, as original as they come, though he never made it in popular theatre. Tom escaped to Yarmouth, but Ben was locked up for six weeks. He was always in hot water. Only a few months later he killed an actor – Gabriel Spencer – in a duel. He could have been hanged, but instead everything he owned was confiscated and he was branded on the thumb to remind him of his lucky escape.

The government threw another obstacle in our way in 1606 with what they called "An Act to Restrain Abuses of Players". We weren't supposed to let any of the characters in our plays use oaths. If they did, we could be fined ten pounds – that's more than some workmen earned in a whole year! Half of the fine was handed over to anyone who informed on us, so of course everyone kept their ears open. I had to make more than 50 changes in *Othello* alone because of this act.

But the greatest obstacle to players was the plague. It caused appalling devastation, sometimes for months – even years – on end. And the government was right to close theatres to try to stop the thing from spreading, but that meant we were on tour even longer than usual – nearly two years, in 1593 and 1594. There were compensations, though. I was able to spend more time with the family, and I took the opportunity to write a couple of long poems which made people realize I could compete with the best of them when it came to classical tales.

I want to ask you about the poems later, but first can you tell me more about the theatre in your early days? You must have had rivals?

I certainly did. Robert Greene was the bitterest. He wrote a little book on his deathbed, which was published by his friend Henry Chettle (another playwright), called *Greene's Groatsworth of Wit*, in which he had the nerve to call me "an upstart crow" and said I thought myself "the only Shake-scene in a country"! But he wrote some rather good plays, such as *Friar Bacon and Friar Bungay* and *James IV*, and I learned something from him about comedy — though not as much as from John Lyly. He was a stylish writer. I couldn't have written some of my early comedies, especially *Love's Labour's Lost*, without Lyly. But he worked only for companies of boy actors, so wasn't a real rival.

The best tragic writers in those early days were Tom Kyd and my dear, reprobate friend Christopher Marlowe. What a character! He was said to have spied in France for the government, he got involved in a forgery scandal and in even more broils than Ben, he was over-fond of boys and tobacco, he blasphemed and cursed – but he wrote like an angel. Lovely poems (*Hero and Leander* gives my *Venus and Adonis* a run for its money), hilarious but tender translations of Ovid, and a succession of wonderful plays. The ones I like best are *Tamburlaine* and *Edward II*. But he was only 29 when he was stabbed to death. We were born within a couple of months of each other, but by his death he'd accomplished far more than I had.

I COULD A TALE UNFOLD

Shakespeare's narrative poem *Venus and Adonis* first appeared in 1593, followed by *The Rape of Lucrece* in the following year. His name appears in full on the title pages, and the poems were well printed. He may have proofread them himself. Each carried a dedication over the author's name to Henry Wriothesley, third Earl of Southampton, who was some ten years younger than Shakespeare. The first dedication is relatively formal, the second much warmer in expression: "What I have done is yours, what I have to do is yours, being part in all I have, devoted yours." These poems were the most frequently reprinted of Shakespeare's writings during his lifetime and well into the later 17th century.

Let's go back to Venus and Adonis. *People are often struck by the fact that when your name first appears in print, it's as a poet rather than a dramatist. How did this come about?*

I'd written about half a dozen plays and was beginning to make a name for myself. Then the horrors of the plague hit the city. Ten thousand Londoners died in 1593 alone. The authorities forbade public gatherings, so the theatres were closed for almost two years. I came back to Stratford, where I wrote my poems.

You had the good fortune to attract Henry Wriothesley as a patron.

Yes, indeed. I really don't think I could have managed without him. We were introduced in

London through a performance I was involved with
at Southampton House, in the Strand. He was 19,
intelligent and exceptionally good-looking — with
what nature might have meant for a woman's face,
and a swathe of auburn hair falling over his left
shoulder. He was kind enough to say he liked my
work, and might I write something for him? He
offered a generous amount of money and asked for
something classical but erotic in verse. I worried that
Venus and Adonis might be too frivolous for him, as I
hinted in my dedication. But he was almost childishly
pleased to be described as the poem's "godfather".
The money he passed my way over those two difficult
years kept my entire family going, and we had
enough left over to pay for my share in the Lord
Chamberlain's Men. And my father — a bit of a snob
— was thrilled to have a son working for a member of
the aristocracy.

It's still thought of as an erotic poem. Could you tell us about that?

Really? Well, that's surprising and pleasing! I suppose I've always believed that people don't change that much in essentials. I took up my old Arthur Golding translation of Ovid – the tale of Atalanta and Hippomenes – and decided to change it so that Adonis was resistant to Venus's advances. The Earl – whose mother was plaguing him to marry, though he felt he didn't know himself well enough to do so – found this most amusing, especially since some of my descriptions of Adonis hinted at the Earl himself. I made sure my old schoolfriend Richard Field printed the poem accurately and elegantly. It took off immediately. Some years later, in one of three plays with Parnassus in the title written and acted by students at Cambridge, one of the characters boasted about sleeping with a copy of *Venus and Adonis* under his pillow. I think I probably facilitated the comfort of many a hot-blooded young man at the time. The same chap said he'd like to have a picture of me in his study! Mind you, he was an absurd fellow.

In contrast, The Rape of Lucrece, *published a year later, was longer and much more serious. Someone has called it "the only joke-free zone" in all your works.*

I'd started it when I came to write the dedication to *Venus and Adonis*. I turned to Ovid again – this time his historical chronicles, the *Fasti*. The politics of Lucrece's rape fascinated me. It took place five hundred years before the birth of Christ. I was keen to emphasize the rapist King Tarquin's banishment at the end, assuming readers would know that Lucrece's rape turned the Roman monarchy into the Roman

Republic. I made my glove-maker father laugh when I have Tarquin pricking his finger on a needle in Lucrece's glove before he goes in to rape her.

But yes, the poem is graver than *Venus and Adonis*, though it became only a little less popular. One is about unrequited love, the other about the destructiveness of a love that's forced. I once met a clever young man called Will Scott, a Member of Parliament, who was flattering about *Richard II*, but bold enough to tell me he'd criticized *The Rape of Lucrece* in his university dissertation about the art of poetry. He said that at least one of my lines was "idle and stuffed". He even quoted the line – slightly inaccurately, I may say – to my face. What I wrote was, "To endless date of never-ending woes." He said I didn't need both "endless" and "never-ending". He was right, of course. He laughed when I corrected his misquotation. The Earl was delighted with the poem, and I meant every word of my loving dedication to him. We became very close.

What effect did the poems have on your subsequent plays?

Richard II came soon after *The Rape of Lucrece*, and Lucrece's grief spilled over into that play. The image of Tarquin struck me years later as a way of describing Macbeth on his way to kill King Duncan. Giacomo in *Cymbeline* recalls Tarquin when in his mind's eye he rapes the sleeping Innogen. And both my Tarquin and Othello (just before he kills Desdemona) express their lust and passion by rolling their eyeballs. Burbage was good at that. And Titania's wooing of Bottom in *A Midsummer Night's Dream* reminded me of *Venus and Adonis*, except that Bottom, unlike Adonis, is only too pleased to be wooed!

IS ALL OUR COMPANY HERE?

Information about Shakespeare's early career
as a playwright is shadowy. He appears to have
written for several companies, possibly starting
as early as 1588. The close relationship between
five of his plays – *King John*, *Henry IV* Parts
One and Two, *Richard III* and *King Lear* – and
various plays performed by the Queen's Men
supports the idea that Shakespeare was at one
time a member of that company. His share in
the founding of the Lord Chamberlain's Men in
1594 was undoubtedly a watershed in his career.
It was a remarkably stable company. Several of
its founders, including Richard Burbage, John
Heminges and Henry Condell (all of whom
Shakespeare mentions in his will), stayed with it
throughout his career and died in its service.

Let's go back to the plays. Can you pinpoint any single event that especially helped you in your playwriting career?

That landmark would be 1594, when Henry Carey, Lord Hunsdon – who was Lord Chamberlain and a great theatre enthusiast – asked some of us who'd worked for several different companies to form a new one, the Lord Chamberlain's Men. The theatres were re-opening after a long spell of plague. It was an honour, but also we needed the work. I was making a reputation as a writer more than as an actor. It was good to join together with the likes of Dick Burbage (who'd triumphed as Richard III), Will Kemp, who'd stepped into Dick Tarlton's shoes as the best natural comic around, and other friends. In the very year we were founded, we played before the Queen, and we gave my *Comedy of Errors* after a Christmas feast before all the aristocratic young lawyers at Gray's Inn – that was a rowdy occasion! We still had to travel around the country at times, but we were lucky enough to be asked to play at court every year.

Hunsdon died in 1596, I think, and for a while Lord Cobham took over as Lord Chamberlain. That was bad news for us because he took great offence at the fact that I'd portrayed an ancestor of his, Sir John Oldcastle, as a fat old rogue in the first of my two plays about King Henry IV. I had to apologize and change the name to Falstaff! But Cobham didn't last long, and within the year the second Lord Hunsdon became Lord Chamberlain. He had a musical mistress called Emilia Lanier who had ambitions as a poet. He had a child by her – I never fancied her myself.

Why was the founding of the Chamberlain's Men so important for you, personally and professionally?

Because of the stability it gave me, both professional and financial. My colleagues trusted me and I was more my own master, choosing the kinds of plays I wanted to write and not having to collaborate with other poets, as I had on *Titus Andronicus* (with George Peele) and on a tedious play about Edward III that I was pushed into helping with. We agreed I should write at least two plays each year, and it was in all our interests that I should ring the changes among comedies and tragedies. Anyhow, I never liked to be too single-minded – some of my plays based on English history have tragic endings, whereas others, especially the ones I wrote between about 1595 and 1600, come much closer to comedy. Audiences found Falstaff so entertaining in the first play I wrote about Henry IV that I put him into a sequel, as well as writing a pure comedy centred on him. That was *The Merry Wives of Windsor*, which had the honour of being played at Windsor before the Queen, who loved it. And *Henry V* ends with marriage bells, just like some of my comedies.

I came to know the particular skills of my colleagues in the Chamberlain's Men inside out, and shaped my plays to suit them. You might almost say that Dick Burbage and I grew up together. In his earlier days he had a fine light touch as a comedian – roles like Biron in *Love's Labour's Lost* and Benedick in *Much Ado About Nothing* suited him perfectly. As time passed, he extended his range, becoming more capable of expressing passion and suffering. He was a wonderfully flexible and intelligent speaker of all kinds of verse, and of prose too. Even quite difficult speeches came trippingly off his tongue. I could trust him with anything from high rhetoric and lyrical verse, like some of Romeo's passionate outbursts, to speeches in verse that nevertheless sound as if the speaker has just made them up, especially Hamlet's soliloquies. *Hamlet* really went down well, with intellectual playgoers as well as with the groundlings. I couldn't have written it without knowing that Dick would play the lead. After that, there was no holding us back – Othello, Lear, Macbeth, Leontes and finally Prospero. We'd sit up late into the night thinking up situations that would show off his talents.

What about the comics?

Will Kemp was the greatest. Audiences would laugh as soon as he came on stage. I had him so much at the forefront of my mind when I was writing the part of Dogberry in *Much Ado About Nothing* that I found myself writing his name in the manuscript instead of the character's – and Richard Cowley's too, who played Verges, his sidekick. I had to be stern with them, though, making sure they didn't say more than I set down for them. Sadly, Will got too big for his boots, and thought he could make it on his own. As a stunt, he morris-danced all the way from London to Norwich. He made a fortune from that, and published a book, *Kemp's Nine Days' Wonder*. He was a restless fellow – travelled to Italy and Germany, but died of the plague in 1603. We were lucky that Robert Armin took over some of his parts. He was more intellectual – short and frail-looking. And he could sing, unlike either Kemp or Dick, so I was able to write parts that were sad, with sad little songs, as well as funny – like Feste in *Twelfth Night* and the Fool in *King Lear*, which I could never have done without him.

Nowadays, one of the things that seems strangest about the theatre in your time is that all the women's parts were played by boys.

Really? It seems perfectly natural to me. Some of them came to us having already been taught to sing and act in choir schools, and it was usual for individual actors to train boys they found promising. Augustine Phillips, for example, had a protégé called James Sands who lived with him and his family. When Augustine died – far too young – he bequeathed to James, who had a lovely voice, his musical instruments. Indeed, he left money to most of his colleagues, even the hired men who came and went as they were needed. And he left me 30 shillings, in gold. I bought a beautiful silver-gilt bowl with it. I handed it down to Judith.

Didn't having boys playing women seem very artificial?

Not at all. Some of the boys were both beautiful and talented. If they weren't, I couldn't have written such demanding parts as Viola and Rosalind. They were played originally by the same lad — lovelier than a summer's day, he was, witty, graceful, full of fun, but with a heart-breaking tenderness to him too. The boy who played Desdemona in Oxford moved the audience to tears simply by the expression on his face in his death scene.

COUNTRY MATTERS

Of Shakespeare's early private life in Stratford and London we know little. For example, only the bare fact of Shakespeare's son Hamnet's burial in 1596 comes down to us. We do know of a letter – which still exists – from Richard Quiney in Stratford addressed to Shakespeare and asking for a loan. And in the manuscript diary of John Manningham we can read the story of Shakespeare's sexual rivalry with Burbage. Shakespeare's connection with the printer Richard Field, mentioned in the following exchange, dates from their schooldays, and we can only assume that the playwright spent time reading on his premises.

*Can we move back to more personal matters? You said
that leaving your family in Stratford was a difficult
decision. Did you ever regret it?*

Frequently, and above all when my only son, Hamnet,
died in 1596. Ironically, that was just a few weeks
before we were granted the family coat of arms,
something my father had wanted for many years. The
boy's death was very sudden, and the news didn't
reach me till he was buried in the churchyard ... but
forgive me, I still can't talk about that without tears.
He was a gallant child.

*I'm sorry, let's take a pause now, and walk around the
garden. It's beautifully maintained ...*

(*Five minutes later, in the garden*) We were talking
about Stratford, and my regrets about leaving. Many

of my colleagues had comfortable homes in London and led a happy family life there, whereas I was all too often on my own, living in lodgings in the capital when we weren't on tour. But Anne couldn't bear to leave Stratford, especially after Hamnet died. She and the girls had many friends there, and my parents and family looked after them, and at least I was able to set them up in style. Theatre was profitable, especially if you had shares in the company, as I did. Only three years after the Chamberlain's Men started business, and a few months after dear Hamnet died, I was able to buy a grand house in Stratford, called New Place. I expect you know it.

Sadly, it was destroyed long ago. All you can see now are the foundations and the garden.

That's a pity. It was one of the finest houses in the

town, close to the Guild Chapel and to my school. It had five gables, and a courtyard with a well in it, and a splendid garden and orchard. It was a bit dilapidated when I bought it, but my father helped to oversee the repairs when I was away, and we soon had it in good shape. I came up to see the family as often as I could, and carried on investing my earnings in property and land here. The townspeople knew they could call on me if they were in need. Some of them often came up to London. Once, when Richard Quincy was staying at the Bell, near St Paul's, he asked me for a loan of £30. Happily, I was in a position to help. It was rather curious because I'd recently written a play about a usurer, called Shylock. But I didn't ask for a pound of Richard's flesh — just a reasonable rate of interest.

Living away from your wife must have brought tensions. I wonder if you know the name John Manningham? He was a member of the Middle Temple, where he saw a performance of your play Twelfth Night, or What You Will on 2 February 1602. Not long afterwards, one of his colleagues told him a funny story about you and Burbage which he wrote down in his diary. It's often quoted — let me read it to you:

"Upon a time, when Burbage played Richard III, there was a citizen grew so far in liking with him that before she went from the play she appointed him to come that night unto her by the name of Richard the Third. Shakespeare, overhearing their conclusion, went before, was entertained, and at his game ere Burbage came. Then, message being brought that Richard the Third was at the door, Shakespeare caused return to be made that William the Conqueror was before Richard the Third."

How scurrilous! But amusing, I admit. We actors were

always subject to that kind of gossip. And it's quite true that some of the women who came to the theatre were liable to take a fancy to us.

There's no truth in the story then?

What else did you want to know, sir?

Sorry … What about your schoolfellows? Did you keep up with any of them?

Oh yes, since my schooldays I'd been friendly with Richard Field, even though he was two years older than me. He got apprenticed to a printer in London, married his master's widow and made a fine career for himself. He was a clever man – printed lots of difficult books on mathematics and subjects like that, as well as poetry by Spenser and Sidney – so I was delighted when he took on my long poems *Venus and Adonis* and *The Rape of Lucrece* in 1593 and 1594. He was a good friend, too. I spent time browsing around his shop, reading and borrowing books such as Holinshed's *Chronicles* and that splendid translation by Sir Thomas North of Plutarch's *Lives of the Greek and Roman Emperors*. As a little private joke I put Richard's name in one of my last plays, *Cymbeline* — it's where I make the disguised heroine say that her name is Richard du Champ. French, you know.

MY LIBRARY WAS DUKEDOM LARGE ENOUGH

Very few of the stories of Shakespeare's plays
are entirely of his own invention. Study of his
sources shows that he made extensive use of the
Bible and classical texts (especially Ovid and
the historical writings of Plutarch), as well as
English historical chronicles, Greek romance,
Italian writings by Boccaccio, Cinthio and
Bandello, and the poetry of Chaucer, Spenser
and (for *Romeo and Juliet*) Arthur Brooke. Even
when Shakespeare appears to have invented
the overall narrative, as in *Love's Labour's Lost*,
A Midsummer Night's Dream and *The Tempest*,
he draws on other writers for episodes and for
details of the dialogue. He obviously saw the
plays and read the work of many contemporary

authors, such as John Florio (1553–1625) (including his translation of Montaigne), John Lyly (c.1553–1606), Christopher Marlowe (1564–93), Robert Greene (1558–92), Thomas Nashe (1567–1601), Ben Jonson (1572–1637) and John Fletcher (1579–1625).

You led a busy life, acting, touring, writing and keeping
up your business interests — but you must have done a
great deal of reading too.

I couldn't have written my plays without that. How
I loved my books! My fellows would spend long
evenings in the tavern following the afternoon
performances, but often I would retreat to my
lodgings and read. I never tired of the great classics
— writers like Ovid and Virgil and Horace, in the
original Latin as well as in translation. And the
English classics, like Chaucer and Gower. More
recent writers, too, such as Spenser and Sidney,
and historians such as Halle and Holinshed. I never
travelled overseas, but there were good translations
of storytellers such as Boccaccio, and I picked
up enough Italian to be able to read Petrarch and
Cinthio in the original — otherwise I couldn't have

written *Othello*. John Florio, who also taught the
Earl of Southampton Italian, as you may know, was
a help there. I got to know Florio personally, as well
as through his books. His remarkable translation
of the essays by Montaigne introduced me to a
kindred spirit I wish I'd discovered earlier. His
was a doubting, questing mind, like Hamlet's. And
his writings came in handy later, when I wrote *The
Tempest*.

Then there were my English contemporaries.
John Lyly was important in the early days because
of his book *Euphues*, but his artificial style soon
went out of fashion, and I even parodied it in one
of Falstaff's speeches. Although Greene was unkind
to me in my early years, I based *The Winter's Tale*
quite closely on his old tale *Pandosto*, and his
coney-catching pamphlets – those short books about
London criminals – gave me ideas for the antics

of Autolycus in the same play. And there was Dr
Thomas Lodge – he was an interesting fellow. In his
early years, he travelled to a country called America
on a voyage during which, improbably, he wrote his
pastoral romance *Rosalynde*, which gave me the story
and many other ideas for my comedy *As You Like It*. I
was delighted to spot him in the audience when that
play was first performed.

Another great playwright, George Bernard Shaw, who
lived hundreds of years after you, praised what he called
your gift of telling a story, provided that someone had
told it to you first. Do you think that was fair?

Witty, but not fair! Obviously in many of my plays
I use historical and other stories that had often
been told before. There was a play about King Lear,
for example, before I wrote mine, and one about

Hamlet, and others about the reigns of King John and Henry V. But writing plays is not simply a matter of telling stories, as your friend ought to know. If this man Shaw took the trouble to compare that old play about Lear – it was printed in 1605 – with mine, he'd see that I transformed it in a manner that made something vastly different – and, if I may say so, a great deal better. None of my plays did I ponder as deeply as that one.

Anyway, there's nothing wrong with re-telling tales that have already been told. Often they're the ones that help us best to understand ourselves. I always enjoyed writing about past times and distant places. Some of my younger colleagues, like Ben Jonson and Thomas Middleton, set their plays in modern London, with sly digs about real people, from the King downwards, but that wasn't my style.

Are there other writers of your time whose work you felt special admiration for?

I mentioned Kit Marlowe — and Thomas Nashe was a favourite too. Eccentric, but brilliant. Try his *The Terrors of the Night* for bizarre originality. You'll find echoes of his *Piers Penniless* in my Henry IV plays. I read a lot of poetry by men like Michael Drayton and Samuel Daniel. And I was fond of Richard Barnfield — perhaps partly because he wrote some kind lines about me quite early in my career! They end like this:

"Live ever you, at least in fame live ever;

Well may the body die, but fame dies never."

That's an idea that lies behind many of my sonnets, as you know. Richard was a great admirer of Kit Marlowe, and they shared the same liking for young men. Richard's love poems are very sweet, and completely open about his tastes, I'm glad to say.

WORDS, WORDS, WORDS

Shakespeare coined numerous words – often
on the basis of Latin, Greek or French – as well
as using language in original ways. Phrases
from his plays pervade modern English. Sayings
such as, "more sinned against than sinning",
"my salad days", "laid on with a trowel" and
"the better part of valour is discretion" are
used in everyday speech with no sense that
they are quotations from Shakespeare. As well
as inventing words he also experimented with
dramatic and poetic form. Only four of his plays
– *Henry VI* Parts One and Three, *Richard II* and
King John – are written entirely in verse. His
use of prose is proportionately greatest in the
middle of his career, up to *As You Like It*, *Hamlet*
and *Twelfth Night*.

Every age has its innovators of language, but what's unusual about you, sir, is that you've come to represent the power of the English language over the last four centuries. It's been calculated that you introduced about 1,700 new words to the language, about half of which are still in use. What was happening to make you coin all those new words?

As many as that? Well, language is like a living creature, it changes constantly, and I was writing at a time of new discoveries. The ships we saw coming up the Thames were laden with the newest and best imports from faraway lands – spices, cloth, precious metals, tobacco ... Hamnet used to love hearing about them ... Merchants and sailors would talk to me about all manner of adventures. They gave me a strong impression of what foreign cities were like, especially Venice. How wonderful this all sounded!

They'd tell me the foreign or new words for things, and I'd think, "I could use this, I could use that."

Then there was my training at the Stratford grammar school. I can think of no better way for the young and developing mind to be creatively stretched than through the study of Latin and Greek. It was as if the very secrets of English were being revealed to me as I studied those languages. They opened the way into French and Italian literature for me too. I remember hearing that most of the books in the Bodleian Library in Oxford were in Latin, and thinking I'd like my native English to be as expressive and powerful as Latin and Greek. The Bible had only quite recently been translated into English, and people of my parents' generation occasionally looked back to the time when Mass was celebrated in Latin – before the new English prayer book came into use. But there was no going back as far as I was concerned. If English had become the language of God, anything was possible. So I took to coining words in order to express the ideas and emotions I wanted to convey.

Sometimes the difficulty of your language puts people off your work. Was that ever so for your own audiences?

I fear it was! And the actors used to complain, "Why can't you just say what you mean, Will, in a more direct way?" My answer always was that if members of the audience were required to step up to the thought, language and feeling in a play, they'd find it a more enriching experience. There was nothing like a sunny afternoon at the Globe when the language was flying, with a heightened feeling of raw human emotion resonating around our wooden O. But there were times when I wanted deliberately to be difficult –

Edgar pretending to be mad in *King Lear*, or Leontes in *The Winter's Tale* becoming totally possessed with jealousy. Equally, though, I liked to offset any sense that I might be over-writing by bringing in some direct, simple language, sometimes out of the blue. A hush would descend when a character suddenly spoke from the heart in a disarmingly simple way. I touched their hearts with my Oldcastle – Falstaff, I mean – in the second part of *Henry IV* when he suddenly says, "I am old, I am old," and with Lear's monosyllables over his dead daughter Cordelia:

"Why should a dog, a horse, a rat have life
And thou no breath at all?"

There seems to have been a rush of prose in your work from the mid-1590s onwards. Why was that?

I suppose I was finding my feet ever more securely

[86]

as a dramatist. Prose flowed from me even more easily than verse. Falstaff was sloshing around the Eastcheap tavern in prose, and in him I found a hitherto unsuspected freedom of expression. *The Merry Wives of Windsor* and *Much Ado About Nothing* contain lots of prose, and it gave playgoers a different kind of music to listen to. I also found that prose fed my use of verse and loosened it up. The Nurse in *Romeo and Juliet* and Hamlet's soliloquies were real breakthroughs I discovered I could produce verse that made it sound as if the speaker were thinking as he spoke – that was exciting. It was a tendency I was able to develop for the rest of my career, especially in my later works.

WHAT THINK YOU OF THIS MAN?

There are numerous references to Shakespeare
in contemporary writings. After the popular
dramatist, poet and prose-writer Robert Greene
described him as an "upstart crow" in 1592,
most allusions are complimentary, and none is
personally derogatory. Shakespeare seems to
have been popular, or at least inoffensive, to his
fellows. The most intimate recollections date
from 1618–19, from Ben Jonson's *Conversations*
with the Scottish landowner and poet William
Drummond (1585–1649). Jonson also provided
the more formal tributes printed in the First
Folio, both in his lines on Shakespeare's
portrait and in his 81-line poem, entitled "To
the memory of my beloved, the author, Master
William Shakespeare and what he hath left us."

You said that your poet friend Richard Barnfield liked your work, but he was referring to your poems. What was your standing as a playwright with the public and with other writers of your time?

I was usually too busy to worry about all that. But, of course, it was important that playgoers liked my work – though they didn't always know it was mine. The playbills often didn't name the authors of plays because, in the early days at least, it was the company that people came to see. But as my reputation grew, especially on account of the popularity of my poems in print, people did come specifically to see my plays. I was unusual because I wrote for the same company for so long, and also because, after the founding of the Lord Chamberlain's Men, I didn't have to collaborate with other playwrights – at least until towards the end of my career.

It's often said today that your audiences were too badly behaved to be worthy of what you gave them. Did you feel that yourself?

Not at all. Audiences could be rowdy at times, especially when the apprentices were on the rampage, and pickpockets and whores were plying their trade in the yard. But you shouldn't believe everything that Puritans like Stephen Gosson and Philip Stubbes wrote about plays and playgoers. Their wrote their attacks on the immorality of the stage years before I came on the scene, and they were shamelessly appealing to the prejudices of their fellow religionists, so it suited their purposes to paint as black a picture as possible. Many respectable and well-educated men and women came to see the plays – people who'd been to grammar schools, like me, and to the universities and the inns of court. Ladies and aristocrats came too. In 1599, after my friends the Earls of Southampton and Rutland had come back from the disastrous expedition to try to quell the rebels in Ireland, they spent most of the summer at the playhouse. And *they* were no fools.

No, I never felt I had to condescend to audiences. Otherwise, how could I have written plays as long and demanding as *Hamlet* – which was the talk of the town for years – and *Othello*, let alone *Coriolanus* and *Troilus and Cressida* (though admittedly that one didn't please the multitude). Some of the plays we put on by other writers went over the audiences' heads. Ben came a cropper with *Sejanus*, which I was responsible for choosing and in which I took one of the leads. I tried to re-write it a bit to make it more palatable, but even so it didn't get beyond its first performance. But what can you expect for a play that includes a long speech translated directly from

Tacitus! You could never tell Ben anything. He sulked for months and had the play printed with a mass of learned notes.

Talking of Ben Jonson, a few years after you died he went on a walking tour to Scotland, where he stayed with a wealthy poet and landowner, William Drummond. They talked late into the night, Ben's tongue loosened, no doubt, by good Scotch whisky. Drummond made notes of what his guest said, and they were published long afterwards. You were one of the main topics of conversation.

How interesting! Let me guess what Ben might have said. Did he by any chance complain that I gave Bohemia a coastline in *The Winter's Tale*? He was nothing if not critical, and loved pointing out that little slip. And he teased me so much about an illogicality in *Julius Caesar* that I rewrote a line. Originally I made Caesar say, "Caesar never did wrong without just cause," which he thought was ridiculous. He had a point, so I changed it to:

"Caesar doth not wrong, nor without cause
　Will he be satisfied."

Not far off! You're right about the first complaint, and he did make the point about Julius Caesar *— in his notebooks, not while talking with Drummond. But Jonson also wrote some very warm things about you, such as saying that he "loved the man, and do honour his memory (this side idolatry) as much as any". And he composed a long poem in your honour in which he called you "sweet swan of Avon" and said you were "Not of an age, but for all time".*

Dear Ben! He had a good heart, for all his carping.

Drank like a fish, and got terribly overweight. You asked what other playwrights thought about me. I had good relations with all of them, I think. I was fond of Thomas Dekker, a hard-working man with a real gift for words – but he could never keep out of debt. His *Shoe-maker's Holiday* is a warm-hearted play. And I got on well with some of the younger writers, like Tom Middleton and John Fletcher. I took John in hand as a young man, and later we wrote several plays together – *The Two Noble Kinsmen* and a rather tedious piece about Henry VIII. And *Cardenio* – that was a nice play. Do you know it?

I'm sorry to say that although we have a few references to it, the play itself hasn't survived.

What a pity! We based it on *Don Quixote*. So it hasn't survived? Dear, dear!

VERY TRAGICAL MIRTH

Shakespeare's plays range widely in subject matter and in tone, and he is notable for the frequency with which he mingles tragedy with comedy, and comedy with seriousness. *Hamlet* is the wittiest of tragedies, and the comedy *Measure for Measure* a deeply serious play of debate that brings several characters close to death. This fusing of genres must, in part, result from a wish to satisfy the demands of a wide range of playgoers, but Shakespeare appears also to have been temperamentally averse to categorization. We do not know if Shakespeare's colleagues exerted pressure on him to write specific kinds of plays, but working for a single company for much of his life must have encouraged his experimentation and search for variety.

How did you choose the subjects for your plays?

It varied. Sometimes my colleagues made suggestions, and I was always looking for ideas in what I read. Then there was the competition. When Kit [Christopher Marlowe] brought out *Edward II*, I thought I could perhaps better that, so I wrote *Richard II*. And his *Jew of Malta* – in which Ned Alleyn was brilliant as Barabas – stimulated me to write *The Merchant of Venice*, with a good part for Dick as Shylock. After Kit died, I missed the challenges he set me. He and his writings haunted my imagination for years! You may realize that he's the "dead shepherd" I mention in *As You Like It*, when I quote a line from his *Hero and Leander*. I don't think I bettered Kit's *Dr Faustus* until I got *Macbeth* out of my system. But the personalities and talents of my actors also gave me ideas for characters and helped me choose what to write, so that, for example, when I read the story of Othello, I knew I could make the central figure a real showcase for Dick Burbage.

How did you manage to write as many plays as you did?

I worked hard! But I wasn't as prolific as some of my fellows – Tom Dekker, for instance, worked on no fewer than nine plays in a single year, whereas I reckoned I'd spread myself too thin if I attempted more than two or, at the most, three. And some subjects, such as King Lear, simmered in my mind for years before I felt ready to put quill to paper. Once I got started I wrote quickly, but the initial reading and the laying out of the plot – and then the polishing when I had a full draft – always seemed to take ages.

You were exceptional among your contemporaries in the

extent to which you blended comedy and tragedy in the
same play. Why did you do this?

Partly because I had good comic actors in my
company and it would have been wasteful not to make
use of their skills. But also because I liked to show
events from a variety of perspectives. Not everyone
approved. I created quite a sensation when the clown
appeared digging the grave in *Hamlet*! Ben was
shocked at the way I flouted classical precedent, but
playgoers greatly preferred my *Hamlet* and *Othello* to
his *Sejanus* and *Catiline*. Yet in *The Comedy of Errors*
all the events take place during a single day in one
market square, which is in line with classical practice
— though even there I introduce the romantic story
about a husband and wife parted in a storm that the
rogue George Wilkins and I told again in *Pericles*.
Then, in the last play I wrote on my own, *The Tempest*,

I even made the events take place in real time, as
the ancients sometimes did. The characters, the
actors and the audience are all no more than about
three hours older by the end.

This will probably be the hardest question of all to
answer, but how did you actually write? What was
your process?

It began before ever I put pen to paper. I had to
choose a subject and then develop a sense of what
I wanted to do and what I wanted to see and hear on
stage. Then I read – a great deal. It was crucial for me
to take an original slant on a story and its characters.
The longest process by far was the planning. A friend
of mine once described it as like building a cathedral.
I wouldn't go as far as that. It was more like a painter
organizing a large canvas so as to make best use of

it. As for the bolts and shackles of ink on paper, I simply needed peace. Not necessarily quiet – hardly ever possible in the family home, and certainly not in London. But in the stillness within me I found the readiness, the ripeness. And then it would pour out. I used to hear it. I saw it taking place in my mind's eye. I could imagine the actors' movements as they played the roles, I could hear the audience's responses. Oh, and I always worked best with the sunlight shining onto the paper as I wrote. I like to think it gave a little extra energy – an added push – to the words themselves.

How far were you influenced by contemporary events?

I was afraid you were going to ask that. All artists write within their time. They see the world as it goes on around them – or at least they should. Chaucer was masterly at that. And so I always sought to honour the great Queen, and afterwards King James – but I wanted to encourage a gently satirical perspective at the same time. For instance, I chose to tell the story of the weak Henry VI, whose succession, like our own Queen's, was insecure, and I made Titania another fairy queen – fall in love with an ass. Then I made Macbeth, like our own King, fascinated with witchcraft and named the villain in *Othello* James (in its Spanish form, Iago).

The worst moment came in 1601, when supporters of the Earl of Essex persuaded the company to perform *Richard II* on the eve of his ill-fated attempt to overthrow Elizabeth. I suppose they thought Londoners would side with the usurping Henry Bolingbroke – who became Henry IV – in toppling the monarch. But I've always felt that at the end of the play audiences feel such sympathy with

the king that they have no time for the usurper.
We were lucky not to suffer for that performance,
and I still feel pangs of guilt when I think about
the execution of Essex, who for all his faults was a
brilliant warrior and statesman – especially when I
recall those lines in *Henry V* where I describe him as
"the General of our gracious Empress" and imagine
his triumphant return to London after his Irish
campaign. That taught me never again to prophesy!

I HAVE A SONNET THAT WILL SERVE THE TURN

Shakespeare's sonnets were first published as a collection by Thomas Thorpe in 1609. The volume bears an enigmatic dedication: "To the only begetter of these ensuing sonnets Mr W H all happiness and that eternity promised by our ever-living poet wisheth the well-wishing adventurer in setting forth. T. T." It is uncertain when the 154 poems were written, whether they are autobiographical, whether any were addressed to real people, and, if so, who these were, and whether Shakespeare wished them to be printed. The following conversation challenges some common assumptions.

A collection of your sonnets was published in 1609, but when did you write them?

I tried to write some sonnets during my youth, but didn't hit my stride until much later. I had the stimulus of a sonnet explosion during the 1590s, set off by the posthumous publication of Sir Philip Sidney's *Astrophil and Stella* in 1591. I was captivated by the demands of the verse structure and the sheer pull of intimacy which it made possible. Gradually, I found I could compress a great deal of thought and feeling into just fourteen lines. I began to think in sonnet form, and it crept into some of my plays. I had fun showing the lords in *Love's Labour's Lost* trying to write sonnets, and making fools of themselves in doing so! *Romeo and Juliet* starts with a sonnet, and the lovers themselves speak a shared sonnet when they first meet. I was pleased with that idea — a good

way of expressing love at first sight. I enjoyed
passing the less intimate of my non-dramatic
sonnets around privately among my friends to see
what they thought of them. They created quite a
stir in some circles towards the end of the 1590s.
One evening I read a few to a party that included a
clergyman called Francis Meres. He called them
"sugared". That was sweet of him!

*Today your sonnets are among the most hotly debated
areas of your entire output. How much of your personal
life is held within them?*

It's difficult to say, apart from those in which I pun
on my first name — I was known as Will, please feel
free to call me that.

Thank you, it's an honour, sir — Will, I mean!

The sonnets weren't all written to actual people, if that's what you're asking. Some were — I wrote some to send home to Anne and the children. But others I wrote originally for my eyes alone. Living in London away from my family wasn't always easy. The city had its temptations — and as you know from my early marriage, I was hot-blooded. In Number 144, I hint that there was a young man who was a great comfort to me, but he got entangled with a faithless woman whom I both loved and hated. And I often felt lonely when we were touring. Late at night I would try to subdue the tumult of my feelings by objectifying them in verse. You'll see what I mean if you read Number 27, the one beginning "Weary with toil, I haste me to my bed."

That's where you write about making journeys in your head. It's among my favourites.

You're a man of taste. There are others that reveal even more of the anguish and sexual torment that assailed me – like Number 151, where I write about sex with an explicitness that shocked some of my readers. There's nothing like it in any other sonnets of the day. I sometimes wonder if I should have allowed that one, and others like it, to appear in print. But they say what I felt, and I care about that.

Some of the sonnets sound to me almost like speeches from your plays. Do you agree?

Yes, I found it useful to produce sonnets on behalf, as it were, of characters I was writing about, like Othello, or Antony, or Cleopatra. Look at Number 108 and imagine it spoken by Antonio, in *Twelfth Night*, to Sebastian. It was a way for me to imagine myself into their inner lives. And then there are the

ones I wrote for the great Earls of Pembroke and
Southampton.

*Otherwise known as Henry Wriothesley and William
Herbert. Is either of them the person you mean by
Mr W. H. in the dedication?*

Good heavens, no! That's not my dedication, anyway.
It's the printer's, Thomas Thorpe's. It would have
been improper to refer to my lords Southampton and
Pembroke publicly as "Mr", however I might have
thought of them in private. Thorpe might have sold
more copies of my sonnets if he'd dedicated them to
an Earl!

Were you responsible for the ordering of the poems?

Of course! It took me ages. Sometimes I made the

ideas within a particular sonnet coincide with its place in the collection. Number 12 starts with a clock ticking through the first line — "When I do count the clock that tells the time ..." I put all those about begetting children at the beginning, which seemed appropriate. I thought it was important to separate all the sonnets clearly addressed to young men (there aren't that many) from those addressed to women (there are even fewer of these). The imagined speaker, the "I", isn't always me, you understand. It's sometimes male, sometimes female, and I didn't always think it necessary to make that clear. Men used to recite to women some of those I'd imagined being spoken by a woman, and vice versa. Now that did make me smile!

READ HIM THEREFORE, AND AGAIN AND AGAIN

Many plays of Shakespeare's time are known by their titles alone: they never appeared in print. Only about half of those that he wrote appeared in his lifetime, and he seems to have had little involvement with their publication. Some – such as the first version of *Hamlet*, in 1603 – were printed from corrupt texts. Others, including the second version of that play, printed in 1604, were taken from the author's own manuscripts. Most of the remainder, along with versions of those that were already published, appeared in the First Folio of 1623. Shakespeare may have started planning this with some of his colleagues in his late years.

As you must know, only about half of the plays you wrote made it into print while you were alive. How did you feel about this, Will?

I was busy acting and helping to run the company, so I wasn't too concerned with print publication. For me, performance was what really mattered. This is one of the ways in which I differed from Ben Jonson. He would write prefaces – often cantankerous – about the way the plays had been acted, and get his friends to write commendatory verses, and so on. I couldn't be bothered with all that – and I didn't even really care that some of my plays were carelessly printed in garbled versions. *Henry V* appeared in 1600 in a short text that even omitted the Choruses. I was especially proud of them, but I did nothing about it. And you wouldn't believe what a mess they made of *King Lear*! That was partly because they got hold of a manuscript in my worst handwriting. I suspect the compositors were half drunk most of the time.

Didn't you ever try to do anything to improve matters?

The time I really got cross was with *Hamlet*. People flocked to see it when it was acted in 1601, with Dick Burbage having his greatest success since Richard III. Then, in 1603, a mangled version was printed – with my name on it. A few of the actors had cobbled it together behind our backs, often making nonsense of what I'd written. Would you believe that "To be or not to be, that is the question" came out as "To be or not to be, ay, there's the point"? That was more than I could bear, so I persuaded my colleagues to join me in a protest. We handed over my original manuscript to the publisher Nicholas Ling, who printed it with the statement that it was "newly imprinted and enlarged to almost as much again as it was, according to the true and perfect copy". After that, we were very cautious in our dealings with publishers.

But after I'd stopped writing plays, I heard that Ben was preparing to publish a volume of his "works", as he called them, and began to think that I could do the same. I knew that some of my best plays hadn't yet got into print. I'm thinking of *Twelfth Night* and *As You Like It* and *Julius Caesar* – Ben was envious of that, even though he quibbled about a couple of lines. And *Antony and Cleopatra* – I don't think I ever wrote finer poetry than in this play – and *Macbeth* and *The Winter's Tale* and *The Tempest*. So I got together with three of my oldest friends and colleagues – Dick Burbage, Henry Condell and John Heminges, "old stuttering Heminges" the audiences used to call him! – and started to plan a rival volume. When I got ill, I made my will and left each of them money to buy mourning rings. I don't know if they ever got around to putting the book together.

I can give you good news there, as I mentioned before! Sadly, Dick died in 1619, but the other two brought together manuscripts of your unpublished plays, compared them with printed texts and with manuscripts held by the company and enlisted the help of Ben and others to write in your praise. They had your portrait engraved as a frontispiece and brought out the volume in 1623. I like to think that your widow may have seen it before she died, in the same year. It did well. The First Folio, as it's known, reprinted three times during the next 50 or so years, and is now one of the most valuable books in the world!

I'm deeply touched to hear that! So Ben's heart softened after all! I'm delighted that people can now read my plays, and above all that they've been made available for performance.

THE WEB OF OUR LIFE IS OF A MINGLED YARN

In the later part of his career, Shakespeare was a well-established playwright and man of the theatre. He maintained a good output of plays, turning away from romantic comedies and English histories to tragedies and tragicomedies (often known as romances). He made a good income, as witnessed by his purchase of property in Stratford, which he clearly regarded as home. He never established a household in London. We know nothing about his financial arrangements with the theatre company – whether he received direct payment for his plays or derived his income from the shares he owned in the company. Certainly, it is unlikely that he profited much, if at all, from the printing of his plays.

Presumably the death of Queen Elizabeth in 1603,
followed by the accession of King James I, was a
milestone in your career.

Yes. We played before the Queen less than two
months before she died, in March 1603. It was
the end of an era, but one good result was that my
benefactor and friend, the Earl of Southampton,
was released from the Tower of London, where he'd
been imprisoned for helping the Earl of Essex in his
abortive attempt to overthrow the Queen. He was
lucky to escape the block. The King's accession was
greeted with bonfires and the ringing of church bells
– and a few weeks later we were thrilled when he gave
us his patronage, which made us indisputably the
leading theatre company, with the right to wear the
royal livery. It was a time of plague, so his coronation
had to be postponed, but when it eventually came, in

March 1604, we each received four and a half yards of scarlet cloth to walk in the procession. But during the Christmas season we had given no fewer than eight court performances, and as the plague was still raging in February, His Majesty generously gave us £30 to help us through the winter. In the following Christmas season, we played at court eleven times, which was a triumph, and I'm proud to say that whereas only two of the plays were by Ben Jonson, seven were by me!

What about your home life during this time?

While I was in London I lived in a succession of respectable but not luxurious lodgings. It wasn't ideal, but it meant that I could send money home to Stratford to keep the family in the style I'd chosen for them. New Place was an expensive establishment to maintain, and I bought a cottage in Chapel Lane for a servant. I also kept up my investments in the town. In 1602, a year after my father died, I bought 107 acres of land, thinking it would make a good marriage settlement for Susanna. I made an even bigger investment in 1605, when I paid £440 for a stake in the town's tithes, which brought in a respectable amount of interest as well as enhancing the family's status. There were sadnesses too. My young brother Edmund, who adored me and who hoped, like me, to make a career in the theatre, died in 1607, aged only 27, leaving a base-born son. I paid for a mourning peal of the bells of St Mary Overy's, close to the Globe, for his burial. All my financial success would have meant more to me if Hamnet had lived, but I hoped that one of my daughters would have sons to keep to keep the family line going. Perhaps you can tell me if that happened?

I hoped you wouldn't ask. I'm sorry to say that Susanna had only a daughter, Elizabeth, whom you knew as a baby. And although Judith had three sons — one of whom she christened Shakespeare in tribute to you, as he was born only seven months after your death — they all died young. The family line died out in 1670.

That grieves me.

I'm sorry. Perhaps we should turn from family to professional matters. What was the next big event in the company's fortunes?

That has to be the opening of the playhouse in the Blackfriars region of London, in 1609. It was the end of a long saga. Dick's father, James Burbage, had bought the property at great expense in 1596, and started converting it as an indoor home for our company to use when the lease on the Theatre expired, in the following year. But local residents – including, would you believe it, our patron the Lord Chamberlain! – objected because they said our drums and trumpets would disturb their Worships' peace and quiet, so the Privy Council vetoed the project. It was leased to a boys' company – I suppose they thought that would be less disruptive – and, in a rather exciting nocturnal expedition which I would tell you about if time were not beginning to press, we moved the timbers of the Theatre across the river to form the Globe. In 1608, the boys' company came into conflict with the authorities and was disbanded, which left the playhouse vacant. Burbage formed a syndicate, of which I was part, to buy it, and after an interval caused by yet another outbreak of plague, we were at last able to open there late in 1609, using it as a winter playhouse. It was a godsend. It was much smaller than the Globe – and roofed, so we could play whatever the weather. We could more easily use spectacular effects, such as flying machinery for Ariel in *The Tempest*, and this affected the way I wrote my late plays, although they still had to be suitable for performing in the Globe.

O SORROW, PITIFUL SORROW – AND YET ALL THIS IS TRUE

During the last seven or eight years of Shakespeare's life, he returned to the practice of collaboration in play-writing, first in *Timon of Athens* with Thomas Middleton, and then in *Pericles* with George Wilkins, who had written a successful play called *The Miseries of Enforced Marriage*. After this, Shakespeare wrote his final solo-authored masterpieces — *Antony and Cleopatra*, *Coriolanus* and *The Tempest*. These were followed by three plays written with John Fletcher: *All is True*, or *Henry VIII*, *The Two Noble Kinsmen* and the lost *Cardenio*. We have no certain knowledge of why Shakespeare collaborated at this point in his career, nor of why he wrote no plays during the last three years of his life.

After you'd kept up a remarkably steady rate of
production for some twenty years, your working habits
seem to have changed around 1607. Why was this?

As usual, it was a combination of happenings.
Partly, I knew I couldn't go on for ever, and I wanted
to encourage up-and-coming writers like Tom
Middleton and my dear young friend John Fletcher.
As I've said, the collaboration with Tom didn't work
out, and we never completed *Timon of Athens*. It
was different with John. He was a delightful young
man, and our minds were more in tune. Like me,
he preferred romantic lyricism to sharp social
satire. He'd been mining a vein of tragi-comedy
that appealed to me, and I thought he could be of
great value to the company for years to come. And
he needed help, having broken up with his partner
Francis Beaumont. They'd lived and written together

for years – they had just one cloak between them and shared the same clothes and bed ... there was a wench around too, but I was never clear what exactly the set-up was. Around 1612, Francis became interested in Ursula Isley – a wealthy woman – which meant he didn't need to write any more. They married in 1613, and poor Francis had a stroke soon after. John was fearfully cut up at the break-up of their *ménage*. That was why I took him under my wing. But what really finished me off was the burning of the Globe, in 1613.

How did that happen?

It was the last Tuesday in June, sunny and warm, and we were putting on *All is True* ...

That's the play called Henry VIII *in the First Folio – I*

suppose to bring it in line with your other plays about
English kings.

Oh, really? Well, *All is True* is what we called it, and it's a much better title for it too. It includes a great scene of the arraignment of Queen Catherine of Aragon, which, by curious chance, actually took place in the very chamber of the Blackfriars that we used for indoor performances. But we put it on beneath the open skies of the Globe because it was one of our most spectacular shows, with fireworks, matting on the stage, extra actors for the coronation scene and lavish costumes – some of them handed down from our aristocratic patrons.

Anyway, it was the second or third performance, and the theatre was packed. All was going well until it came to the scene where the king puts on a masque to impress Anne Boleyn. We really worked up the

spectacle with fireworks and cannon fire! The
guns were behind the theatre, and of course they
were firing blanks, but a foolish extra must have
allowed some of the wadding in the cannon to get
loose, and it fell on the thatch. At first there was just
a tiny wisp of smoke, and no one took it seriously –
all eyes were on the actors – but it must have burned
under the surface, and before long there was an
almighty blaze. The actors fled the stage and people
began to leave the theatre through every possible
opening. One poor fellow's breeches caught fire –
he put it out with a bottle of ale he'd just bought
(rather a waste, you might think). Another was
scorched when he nobly went back into the yard
to rescue a poor child whose parents had left him
behind. By enormous good fortune we managed to
save the playbooks – what a disaster if those had
been swallowed up! – and most of the costumes.

All we lost was a few old cloaks which we could well do without.

So it could have been worse!

Yes, but it hit us hard. We all loved that building! We'd carried the timbers over the river to Southwark in 1599 to build it, we'd worked there for fourteen years, and some of my best plays – *Hamlet*, *Twelfth Night, or What You Will*, *King Lear* – had been put on there for the first time. And it was a terrible financial loss. Some fool of a ballad-maker wrote a song that was sung all over the city within hours, saying that if we rebuilt the theatre we should tile the roof instead of thatching it. He was right, of course, and that's what we did. In fact we had a new theatre up within a year. But it nearly broke my spirit, and I didn't write any plays single-handed after that.

I'm pleased to be able to tell you that nearly four hundred years later, a new, reconstructed Globe has been built close to where the original stood. Your plays are put on there to thousands of people every summer.

Wonderful! Tell them to be careful of cannon fire!

What did you do after that?

I started to spend more time in Stratford, though I still went down to London from time to time. There were some sad happenings. My two remaining brothers died — Gilbert in 1612 and Richard the following year. I was involved in trouble over the enclosure of land I owned at Welcombe, just outside Stratford, and then there was a miserable scandal about Thomas Quiney, the man my daughter Judith married in 1616. I changed my will because of that

— and I got ill, and, well, probably you know more
about what happened after that than I do!

NOW MY CHARMS ARE ALL O'ERTHROWN

None of Shakespeare's private papers survives. We have no letters written by him, no diaries and no recollections by any member of his family. However regrettable this may be, it is not surprising. Most of what we know about William Shakespeare has to be extrapolated from his writings. Of these, the sonnets appear to be the most personal. In his plays, Shakespeare is so much "the chameleon poet" – a phrase coined by one of his finest readers, the poet John Keats – that it is exceptionally difficult to identify his own point of view. Each reader and playgoer forms his or her own impression of the mind and personality that lie behind the work.

How we wish we had some autobiographical writings of yours, or even some non-fiction!

I never thought that posterity would take much interest in me as a person. It was my work I cared about. A man's private life – his inner life – remains private in the end, whether he leave personal papers or not.

Which plays are you most fond of?

It's hard to choose. I enjoyed making people laugh, as in the eavesdropping scenes in *Love's Labour's Lost* and *Twelfth Night, or What You Will*. I liked it, too, when I knew I'd broken a mould and challenged expectations – such as the ambivalence of Hamlet's intentions or the death of Cordelia at the end of *King Lear*. It was good when my poetry stilled the house, and when scenes of recognition held audiences spellbound. *Antony and Cleopatra* was my most ambitious work – lots of sudden scenes spread over three continents, with poetry and humour underpinning everything. My account of Falstaff's death could draw tears, but perhaps most moving of all was the close of *The Winter's Tale*. When the supposed statue of Hermione comes to life and she sees her husband and daughter for the first time in sixteen years – the way all three are changed by what time has done to them ... what can I say? Anne said it was her favourite, and that makes me especially fond and proud of it.

That's touching. Your life was fulfilled in your works.

And in my family too. Hamnet's death was the saddest moment of my life ... but one simply goes on. And

I'm pleased that my dear parents saw how well
I'd done.

On your monument in the sanctuary of Holy Trinity
Church here in Stratford, the lines in Latin say that
you were "a Nestor in counsel, a Socrates in mind,
and a Virgil in art". How would you most like to be
remembered?

That's praise indeed. And in the sanctuary! Probably
Ben Jonson's influence, all those classical names.
Nestor seems like a backhanded compliment,
though. He's rather absurd in *Troilus and Cressida*,
though well respected. I suppose the idea is that
I was a good listener. I used always to be cautious
about giving advice that might seem impertinent,
even though people would seek me out and take me
into their confidence about all manner of things.

Sex, quite a lot of the time. People get too worked up about that. Socrates? I suppose that generously relates to the way I always thought in dialogue, and believed in the power of the word to change and shape the world. Virgil? Goodness only knows! I was fascinated in the supernatural possibilities of the ordinary – but the mantle seems too grand. I suppose in the end I'd like to be remembered for having taken my Stratford with me into whatever I was writing about   the country lore of my childhood, the Warwickshire I knew and loved. I made money, bought a fine house, acquired a coat of arms, raised a family and entertained many people with both the printed and the acted word. There's little more to say than that.

There's much more, Will, that I should like both to ask and to tell you, but I've kept you for too long. It's been a wonderful privilege to talk with you. Had we but world enough and time, I could tell you more wonders and no doubt you could repay me a hundredfold!

NOTES

Quotations from the works of
William Shakespeare are from *The
Oxford Shakespeare: The Complete
Works*, edited by Stanley Wells et al.
(Oxford: Oxford University Press,
1986)

(UN)WILLINGLY TO SCHOOL
p.30 (Un)willingly to school
As You Like It, 2.7.147
PLAY THE MAN I AM
**p.38 Rather say I play/The man
I am** *Coriolanus*, 3.2.14–15
p.42 I hate ... 'Not you'. *Sonnet*
145
BY MY TROTH, WELCOME TO
LONDON
**p.45 By my troth, welcome
to London** *Henry IV Part Two*
2.4.294–95
I COULD A TALE UNFOLD
p.52 I could a tale unfold *Hamlet*,
1.5.15
p.56 the only joke-free zone
Katherine Duncan-Jones, *Ungentle
Shakespeare: Scenes from his Life*
(London, 2001), p.73
**p.57 To endless date of never-
ending woes** *The Rape of Lucrece*,
1.935

IS ALL OUR COMPANY HERE?
p.59 Is all our company here?
A Midsummer Night's Dream, 1.2.1
COUNTRY MATTERS
p.68 country matters *Hamlet*,
3.2.111
**p.72 Upon a time, ... before
Richard the Third.** *The Diary
of John Manningham of the Inner
Temple*, 1602–3, R.B. Sorlien (ed.)
(Hanover, New Hampshire, 1976),
p.202
MY LIBRARY WAS DUKEDOM
LARGE ENOUGH
**p.75 my library was dukedom large
enough** *The Tempest*, 1.2.109–10
**p.81 Live ever you, ... but fame
dies never.** Richard Barnfield, "A
Remembrance of Some English
Poets"
WORDS, WORDS, WORDS
p.82 Words, words, words *Hamlet*,
2.2.195
p.86 I am old, I am old *Henry IV
Part Two*, 2.4.273
**p.86 Why should a dog, ... no
breath at all?** *King Lear*, 5.3.282
WHAT THINK YOU OF THIS MAN?
p.88 What think you of this man?
Troilus and Cressida, 3.3.254

p.93 Caesar doth not wrong, …**Will he be satisfied.** *Julius Caesar*, 3.1.47–48

p.93 loved the man, … as much as any Ben Jonson, from his notebooks published in 1630 as *Discoveries*

p.93 sweet swan of Avon Ben Jonson, "To the Memory of my Beloved, the Author, Master William Shakespeare", l.71

p.93 Not of an age, but for all time Ibid, l.43

VERY TRAGICAL MIRTH

p.95 very tragical mirth *A Midsummer Night's Dream*, 5.1.57

p.96 dead shepherd *As You Like It*, 3.5.82–83

p.102 the General of our gracious Empress *Henry V*, 5.0.30

I HAVE A SONNET THAT WILL SERVE THE TURN

p.103 I have a sonnet that will serve the turn *The Two Gentlemen of Verona*, 3.2.92

READ HIM THEREFORE, AND AGAIN AND AGAIN

p.110 read him therefore, and again and again *Epistle to the First Folio* by John Heminges and Henry Condell

p.112 To be or not to be, that is the question *Hamlet*, 3.1.58

THE WEB OF OUR LIFE IS OF A MINGLED YARN

p.116 The web of our life is of a mingled yarn *All's Well That Ends Well*, 4.3.74–75

O SORROW, PITIFUL SORROW – AND YET ALL THIS IS TRUE

p.123 O sorrow, pitiful sorrow – and yet all this is true "A Sonnet upon the Pitiful Burning of the Globe Playhouse in London"

NOW MY CHARMS ARE ALL O'ERTHROWN

p.131 Now my charms are all o'erthrown *The Tempest*, Epilogue, 1

p.131 the chameleon poet John Keats, from a letter to Richard Woodhouse, 27 October 1818

REFILL?

OVERVIEWS

Andrew Dickson's *The Rough Guide to Shakespeare* (London: Rough Guides, 2005) is an excellent all-round compendium – well-informed, critically astute and agreeably written. It may be complemented by *The Oxford Companion to Shakespeare*, edited by Michael Dobson and Stanley Wells (Oxford: Oxford University Press, 2001), an illustrated encyclopedia covering all aspects of the subject. Among websites, those of The Shakespeare Birthplace Trust (www.shakespeare.org.uk) and the British Shakespeare Association (www.britishshakespeare.ws/) provide useful up-to-date information and links.

BIOGRAPHIES

Of the many available, especially recommended are Park Honan's *Shakespeare: A Life* (Oxford: Oxford University Press, 1998), Michael Wood's *In Search of Shakespeare* (London: BBC Books, 2003), which complements his series of television programmes, and Stephen Greenblatt's *Will in the World* (New York: Norton, 2004). The case against Shakespeare is presented in Katherine Duncan-Jones's well-informed and sharply written *Ungentle Shakespeare: Scenes from his Life* (London: Thomson Learning, 2001).

Shakespeare: For All Time (London: Macmillan, 2002), by Stanley Wells, offers discussion of Shakespeare's life, his methods of work, and his afterlife up to 2000. James Shapiro's *1599: A Year in the Life of William Shakespeare* (London: Faber and Faber, 2005) is a fascinating study of a (long) year in Shakespeare's life. *Shakespeare's Sonnets* by Paul Edmondson and Stanley Wells (Oxford: Oxford University Press, 2004) provides an overall study of these poems, which are enigmatically relevant to Shakespeare's biography.

INDEX